LEARNING ABOUT Trees

Catherine Veitch

Raintree

Chicago, Illinois

The author would like to dedicate this book to her mother, Jacqueline Veitch, who inspired her with a love of nature.

© 2014 Raintree
an imprint of Capstone Global Library, LLC
Chicago, Illinois

To contact Capstone Global Library please phone 800-747-4992, or visit our website www.capstonepub.com

Edited by Dan Nunn, Rebecca Rissman, and Sian Smith
Designed by Joanna Hinton-Malivoire
Picture research by Mica Brancic
Production by Sophia Argyris
Originated by Capstone Global Library Ltd

Library of Congress Cataloging-in-Publication Data
Veitch, Catherine.
Learning about trees / Catherine Veitch.—1st ed.
p. cm.—(The natural world)
Includes bibliographical references and index.
ISBN 978-1-4109-5402-2 (hb)
ISBN 978-1-4109-5407-7 (pb)
1. Trees—Juvenile literature. I. Title. II. Series: Natural world (Chicago, Ill.)
QK475.8.V45 2013

582.16—dc23   2012049393

Acknowledgments
The author and publisher are grateful to the following for permission to reproduce copyright material: Alamy: Bob Gibbons, 4 top right, REDA & CO srl, 8; FLPA: Adri Hoogendijk/Minden Pictures, 19 top right, Bob Gibbons, 4 left, Derek Hall, 16 left, Marcus Webb, 8 inset, 19 bottom right, Martin B Withers, 5 bottom left; Nature Picture Library: Mike Read, 9, Simon Colmer, 16 bottom right; Photoshot: NHPA/Kevin Schafer, 12, Photos Horticultural/Michael Warren, 20; Shutterstock: Alessandro Zocc, 18, 18 inset, 23 (cone), Badon Hill Studio, 15, Bobkeenan Photography, 24 (seeds), Brandon Bourdages, 15 inset, 23 (fruit), Chuck Cho, 5 middle, EastVillage Images, 7, 22 (bark), 24 (trunk), Ewa Studio, 5 top right, 22 (blossom), Frank L Junior, 21 inset, Grigorii Pisotsckii, 4 bottom right, haraldmuc, 22 (bud), Jeff Dalton, back cover, 21, Julie Simpson, 12 inset, Konrad Weiss, 17, 22 (branch), kosam, 14, Maksym Gorpenyuk, 11, 24 (roots), marilyn barbone, 19 left, marlee, 9 inset, 22 (berry), Martina I. Meyer, 10 left, Nastya22, 14 inset, Oleg Znamenskiy, 6, Photodigitaal.nl, 20 inset, 23 (flower), Radka Palenikova, 10 bottom right, 23 (leaf), Robyn Mackenzie, 17 inset, Sergej Razvodovskij, 16 top right, 23 (catkin), sonya etchison, cover, Tamara Kulikova, 7 inset, Tolchik, 10 top right, William Berry, 13 inset, 24 (pine needles), Zack Frank, 13

We would like to thank Michael Bright for his invaluable help in the preparation of this book.

Contents

Ash

Cherry

Dragon's Blood

Giant Sequoia

Hazel

8

Holly

Horse Chestnut

Mangrove

Monkey Puzzle

North American Pine

13

Oak

Pear

Pussy Willow

Silver Birch

Spruce

American Sycamore

Tulip Tree

20

Weeping Willow

Picture Glossary

bark rough, outer covering of a tree

berry small, round fruit with one seed or lots of seeds inside

blossom flowers that appear on a fruit tree before the fruit

branch part of a tree that grows out of the tree's trunk. Branches help a tree spread its leaves out.

bud part of a plant that grows into a new leaf or a flower

catkin small group of flowers on a short stem that grows on some trees

cone hard case that keeps seeds safe. Fir and pine trees have seed cones.

flower part of a plant that makes seeds. The smells flowers make and their colors help attract insects.

fruit fruits hold seeds. Plants make fruit so that animals will eat the fruit and carry the seeds to new places.

leaf part of a plant. Leaves use sunlight to make food for the plant.

pine needles long, thin, pointed leaves

roots part of a plant that holds the plant in the ground. Roots bring water to the plant.

seeds plants make seeds. Seeds grow into new plants.

trunk main stem of a tree

Notes for Parents and Teachers

- Go on a nature walk with the children. Help them identify different trees and their parts. Explain that trees are a type of plant. The children can sketch or photograph what they see. Use the pictures to make a class book.
- Collect different leaves and make some bark rubbings. Discuss the different shapes and colors of leaves, and the different bark patterns. Add the pressed leaves and bark rubbings to the class book. Remind children to always check with an adult that leaves are safe to collect, and to always wash their hands after handling leaves.